Goodbye America

A Great-Grandmother's Personal Childhood Story

Rita Malie

Goodbye, America
A Great-Grandmother's Personal Childhood Story
by
Rita Malie

Published and distributed by:
High-Pitched Hum Publishing
321 15th Street North
Jacksonville Beach, FL 32250

www.highpitchedhum.net

High-Pitched Hum
Publishing

Dustjacket and layout design by Betty Tuininga
Edited by Mary Yee and Nicole L. Kradjian

Cover Art by the 19th Century French Artist
Adolphe William Bougereau, 1891, Oil on canvas

ISBN Number: 978-0-9787995-7-1

Printed in the United States of America

Dedication

I dedicate this book to my mother, Anna, who remained ever grateful for living in a free country. She taught three generations of our family that the human spirit has the strength to maintain hope and faith in the face of extraordinary adversity.

Acknowledgements

There are five people who played crucial roles in making this book possible and I wish to thank them with all my heart. Pat Hoyt and Janet Walter are two friends who willingly offered literary guidance in my writing development. My sister, Michele DeBacco, a gifted teacher, provided the valuable educational adjuncts. Dr. Lubor Matejko, Department Head of Russian Language and Literature at Comenius University, Bratislava, Slovak Republic, never hesitated in providing the research necessary to ensure the book's historical accuracy. Lastly, I want to thank my loving husband, Nick, for his continued patience and understanding seeing me through the completion of this labor of love.

Chapters

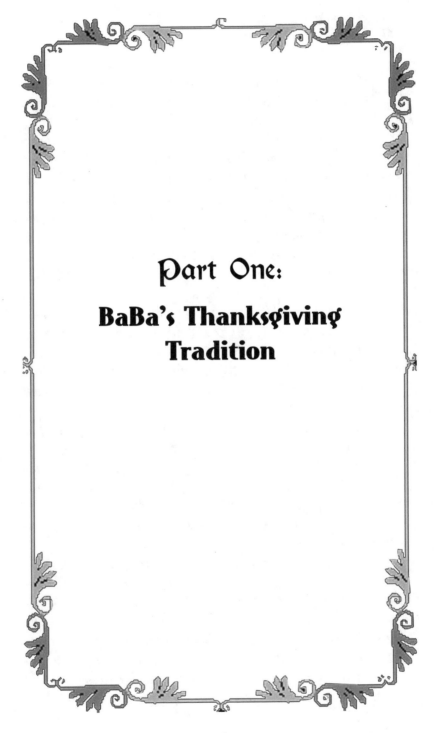

Part One:

BaBa's Thanksgiving Tradition

Straightening the pictures of her family on the shelf, Anna looked at the photographs from the past and those from the present. Balancing herself against her walker, she wiped away a tear as she stared at those faces from the past, holding each faded, wrinkled picture. The tiny age cracks and washed out sepia colors in the photos were not much different than the veins in her dry, sallow and spotted hands. She felt so old just thinking of all the changes she'd seen and how she survived her childhood.

As she looked at each picture, she thought of how much people change, but photographs never really grow old. Her Mommo and Deddo looked so serious in their wedding picture. Who knew then that Deddo's dream of making a better life would be cut short, dying from the flu epidemic just four years after his family joined him in America? Everyone looked so sad, standing side-by-side like soldiers; so stiff, yet never touching or smiling. Their grim faces looked like someone was ready to march them out to a firing squad. There was no reflection of happiness or hope in their eyes. Julia, the youngest of four children, died at fourteen from pneumonia. George, spoiled because he was the only boy, and Mary, sweet and loving Mary, who was the substitute mother for all of them. Her love taught us that there's always a rainbow of happiness within our reach.

Now, Anna was alone again. Sisters, brother, parents were gone. She loved to reminisce about the happy as well as the sad times when her family was still alive. As she straightened the photographs of her two loving Great-Granddaughters, Morgan and Madison, she noticed the differences between the faces from the past and those of the present. Dressed in bright, vivid and colorful clothes, their young faces expressed Cheshire cat-like smiles. They cuddled her in each picture. She was grateful her family traveled from many different states to celebrate Thanksgiving with her every year.

2

She was startled with several hard knocks on the door and little voices shouting, "Are you there, BaBa?"

"Nazdar, moje anjels [1] (Hello, my angels), I'm coming." Anna moved slowly with her walker to the front door. As soon as she opened it, they engulfed her with bear hugs and kisses.

"BaBa," they cried, "We missed you. Do you have any treats?"

"No, moje anjels, not yet. I don't want to spoil your appetites with treats. The turkey will be done soon. Is everyone downstairs?"

"Yes, BaBa," said Morgan. "We were the last to get here."

"You girls are growing faster than that maple tree outside my window. What's your mother feeding you these days, plant food?"

"BaBa, you always say that," said Madison, as she rolled her big brown eyes, tugging at BaBa's arm while searching the apartment for any noticeable changes. "You're silly."

Anna couldn't believe how much the girls had grown. Her heart warmed as she carefully took the time to notice how they changed from the year before. Even though the girls were only two years apart, their spirits and features were vastly different. Morgan had a deep dimple on her left cheek and was tall and slender like a beautiful willow tree. Even at eight years old, she was very intuitive and never impulsive, always knowing when and how to warm up to her BaBa. She had a habit of biting her nails whenever she felt tense and unsure of herself.

Madison, on the other hand, was overconfident and spontaneous. Truly the actress, she was extremely animated and expressive. She always threw herself into BaBa's lap knowing her love and warmth would be returned.

Although Anna's apartment was one floor above the kitchen at the assisted living complex, the smell of turkey began to fill the house. The delight of another Thanksgiving holiday could not be mistaken as the delicious aroma of pumpkin pies spread throughout the entire building. The girls enjoyed exploring BaBa's small apart-

Madison, Anna, and Morgan

ment. *They liked to pretend the entire building belonged to her and always called it 'BaBa's Big House.' They loved jumping in her vibrating lounge chair that the family bought her last Christmas. Running to the picture shelf, they once again asked about the past.*

"BaBa, your pictures look so strange. They have no color. They're all black, white and brown. And why do the girls wear those ugly babushkas *(head covering)? Why doesn't anyone smile in your pictures and what are the funny white dresses those girls are wearing?"*

"Those are Communion dresses. My sisters, Mary, Julia and I all had our First Holy Communion together." It's as if time had stood still and nothing changed for seventy-seven years as she looked at that picture. "We treasured those dresses, feeling like beautiful grown up brides on our special day. Won't you soon be celebrating your Holy Communion this year Morgan? I'll bet your Mother will buy you a beautiful white dress. Then you'll know what it feels like to be a princess, admired by everyone."

"BaBa, how old are you now?" They asked her that every year.

"Soon, I'll be eighty-nine, moje anjels."

"BaBa, please tell us that story again about how that snake

4

Mary, Julia, and Anna – First Holy Communion, 1926

bit you and you screamed so loud that the whole village heard you! Is this how loud you screamed, AH-H-H!?" yelped Madison.

"Hush, Madison!" said BaBa. "You'll wake the dead with that scream. Everyone downstairs will think something dreadful has happened!"

"You're so dramatic, Madison," Morgan chimed in.

Ignoring her big sister, she continued, "Show me your scar where the snake bit you, BaBa. Show me your scar. I want to kiss it. Your leg swelled up how big? As big as a beach ball?" Madison curled her arms into a big circle to demonstrate the size of her swelling. "And your Great-Grandpa, didn't he suck out the poi-

son? Yuk!"

"But that's what saved BaBa's life, Madison," said Morgan. "That and the hot horse manure."

"And how long was it before you could go to school? A year? Please! Please! BaBa, tell us your story again. That's the best part of our visit."

"I'd like to hear the part where you had to say goodbye to your Deddo and America." Morgan softly put her hands around BaBa's face stroking her pale cheeks. She looked into her eyes and pleaded for the story to be told one more time. "They haven't even set the table for us downstairs," said Morgan. "I know we have plenty of time."

"Well, all right girls. You know Thanksgiving is such a special day for me to spend with you and tell you my story. This is the day for us to remember how thankful we are for all our blessings and to be living in America."

Anna began telling her story...

America, 1918

My parents were born in a landlocked country in the heart of Europe called Slovakia. It was mainly a farming country made up of more than three thousand little villages. Slovaks were very proud to grow the corn that fed their people and farm animals. Other types of businesses were very slow to develop in the early 1900s.

Slovak schools were taken over by a foreign people called Magyars.[2] They were the controlling group of people from a neighboring country called Hungary. Magyars held power over the Slovak people, and forbid them to use their language in books and newspapers. They even closed their schools and churches. People weren't free to speak or write in their own language.

Magyars threw Slovak leaders into prison. Slovaks didn't have basic human rights that Americans had already been enjoying for over one hundred fifty years. Nearly one million Slovaks began leaving their homes between 1850 and 1921, looking for a better life for their families. America promised to be a land of opportunity, offering prospects they never had in their country. In 1910, more Slovaks moved to America than any other European nationality.[3]

In America, they quickly built their own schools, churches and social organizations. Slovak Americans were kept informed of homeland news by their newspaper, *Jednota*, which is published to this day. Many of them came to America without any special skills and found jobs in the mines and steel mills in the Midwest.[4] That's how we settled in Ohio, where I live 'till this day.

7

My Deddo, Karl, was a handsome, tall, loving man. He had a broad, square face and prominent chin that matched his confident stride. He was determined to make his way in America. Over and over he preached to Mommo, "Maria, we cannot stay here and raise our family where freedom to think and act is forbidden. I promise you, moving to America will bring happiness to our lives. I know I can make a better life for you and the children in America."

Mommo, who was slightly built and small enough to stand under Deddo's outstretched arm, didn't want to leave her family and country. That's all she knew. She had no desire to venture to another strange land. She soon gave in, shaking her fist at him, exclaiming, "All right, Karl, go to America...but promise me if things don't work out, you'll come back. You think you can conquer the world, but I'm not sure you can."

So, my Deddo left Slovakia in 1912. He settled in Ohio, in a little town about twenty miles from here. He learned about blast furnaces and found a job in a steel mill. He earned enough money in two years to send for Mommo, Mary and George. Shortly after the family got settled, Julia and I were born.

We lived with many other Slovak immigrants in a crowded neighborhood where we were able to keep our language and culture alive. Adults continued to speak Slovak, but the children soon began speaking English and learning American ways while they attended school.

Shortly after our family got settled, tragedy struck.

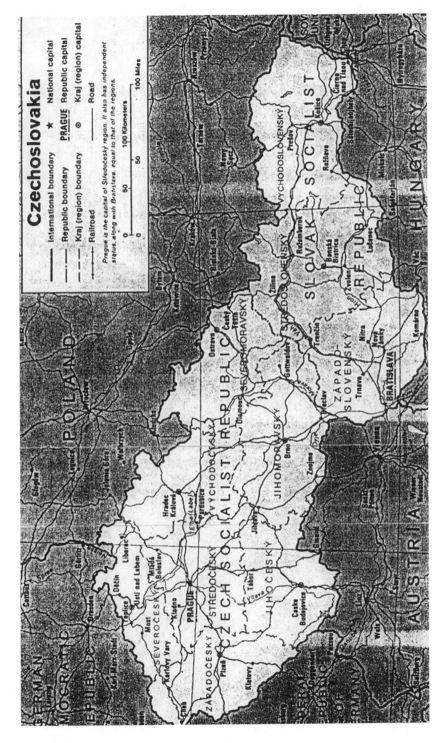

9

Goodbye, Deddo and America

The year was 1918. World War I had just ended. The flu epidemic began during the war and was still infecting and killing people a year later. People in all parts of the world were affected—Spain, France, Germany, China, Japan, America, Africa and India. Over seventy million people died throughout the world. Almost every family in America had someone sick with the flu. Many of them died within days. About 850,000 Americans died from the flu in less than two years.[5]

One day when Deddo, Julia and I were sick with the flu, Mommo went next door to see if our neighbors were all right. She was worried since she hadn't seen them for a while. She ran home yelling, "They're all dead! They're all dead!"

"Who's all dead?" cried Mary.

I grabbed Julia and we both ran and hid under the bed in the next room. Mommo scared us. Mary was the brave one. She always took over when Mommo lost control.

It took some time for Mary to calm her down. Finally she was able to talk again.

"They're all dead next door—mother, father, and both children. When is this terrible illness going to be over? Who's going to die next?"

A few nights later I woke up to the sound of crying. The doctor came to our house. We all were getting sicker from the flu. When he finished examining us, he looked at Mommo over his glasses that perched low on his nose and told her the bad news. "Anna will live, but your husband won't live through the night."

Mommo screamed, "It can't be true!" Throwing her hands in the air, she looked and pointed at me with an unsteady finger and cried, "Why can't God take *you*, Anna, instead of your father?"

I'll never forget the look in her eyes when she shouted those words. She was like a stranger who intends to strike at an enemy. Although I didn't understand everything that was happening then, somehow I knew what she meant. I knew I must've done something terribly wrong. I sobbed. Her words stabbed me deep in my heart. She didn't love me. There was nowhere to hide. I was too weak to run away. I melted into the side of my bed, never wanting to look at her again. My body shook from fear. I didn't know what she would do next.

Mary tried to console me, "Don't cry, Anna. Mommo didn't mean it."

I knew she meant it. She didn't love me anymore. I was scared of her. I was afraid to look at her eyes. I stayed away from her. I didn't want to remind her it was my fault that Deddo was sick. She never looked at me again. She knelt at his bedside praying throughout the night.

Mary rocked me in her arms crying over and over, "Mommo loves you, Anna. She's just heartbroken. We're all sad about Deddo."

But Mommo never changed her words. Years later, she repeated those words over and over, blaming me for Deddo's death. I feel sad whenever I remember the look in her eyes and how her words cut into my heart. They hurt more than any whipping could.

Mary said Deddo was dying. I didn't know what that meant. Would Julia and I die too? Did we do something to make Deddo sicker? I remember we were so hot from fever that Mary kept putting cold cloths on our heads to cool us down. Later, we would be so cold that we would shiver and beg for warm blankets. What was this terrible illness that caused people to die? Why didn't I die? I didn't understand what was happening. We didn't know how this illness was going to change our lives...or how bad things were going to get.

The next morning, I woke up feeling groggy and saw Deddo lying in a casket downstairs in the living room. Everyone was crying.

"What happened, Mary?" I asked.

"Hush, Anna. You know how sick Deddo was. He died last night," she whispered in a low weepy voice so close to my ear that it tickled me with her wet tears. "You need to be quiet, and take care of Julia. I don't have much time to talk because lots of people will be coming to the house. George and I need to help Mommo. She just cries and keeps saying, "What am I going to do with *moje sirotky* (my little orphans)?"

"You be good and keep Julia quiet. Call me if you need anything. Don't bother Mommo. You'll have to be a big girl now." She kissed my cheek and rubbed my elbow. Mary always did that whenever she knew I was scared or unhappy. She grabbed some milk and oatmeal, poured everything into two bowls: one for Julia, and one for me. She quickly left the kitchen. I choked. I felt a big lump in my stomach. I couldn't eat that morning, or for the rest of the day.

I wondered why she said don't bother Mommo. I never bothered her anyway. She was always too busy for Julia and me. She always yelled and shouted a lot. I could never understand why she was so unhappy. Deddo was the happy one. He always softened her up by calling her *moja mila* (my sweetheart). That always teased a smile from her hard mouth that was usually pursed tightly like she just ate something sour.

Now Deddo was gone. Mommo wanted to be with her family again, who were thousands of miles away.

Later that night while everyone was asleep, I tiptoed

Anna, Mommo, Mary, Deddo, and George

into the living room to talk to Deddo. I walked slowly to his casket. At first I was scared because the room was so dark, but I always knew whenever I was with him, I would be safe. He looked so gray and sad. I don't ever remember him ever looking that sad before. He was lying in a dark brown box that was draped in a white cotton cover that hung over the sides almost touching the floor. He was dressed in a black suit that he always wore to church on Sunday. His shirt was wrinkled. As I got closer, I felt the roughness of his cheek from his beard and smoothed his hair. I touched his folded hands which were cold and hard. The room was cold and damp and smelled musty. The casket sat in front of the window where the reflection of the moon cast shadows on his face. I climbed up on a chair to talk to him and laid my head in his lap.

"Deddo, I prayed to God tonight. I asked him if I could die and you could come back. I told God how sad Mommo was and that Mary, George and Julia needed you. Deddo, if you'll wake up, I'll take your place in that box. It's okay, I'm not scared."

I waited a long time for something to happen. I waited

for such a long time for Deddo to wake up that I fell asleep. But he never woke up. God didn't bring him back and take me in his place. I kissed his rough cheek and said goodbye. Would Mommo ever forgive me? Would she ever smile again?

Now Mommo was a widow with four children to care for. How would she take care of her four orphans? My Deddo worked and earned money. Mommo stayed home and cared for her family. There was no one to help her and she was terrified. Her family lived far away in another country, across the Atlantic Ocean. She longed to be with them. She was sure things would be better if she could just go home. So, she sold everything we owned. She made all the arrangements and collected the necessary government papers. She didn't know what we would be facing when returning to Europe after a World War had just been fought there.

So, I said goodbye to Deddo and now I was saying goodbye to America.

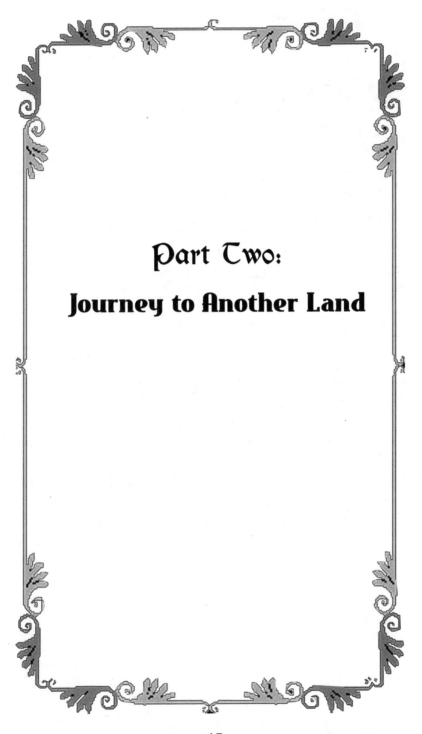

Part Two:

Journey to Another Land

"*Do you remember the next part of my story, moje anjels?*" "*When our family made the long trip back to Mommo's village, everyone there was trying to overcome the hardships and other challenges they faced that were brought on by the war.*"

Morgan noticed BaBa's eyes filling with tears. "*I'd cry just like you if my Daddy died and I had to move away from my home and friends.*"

"*Well, some of my tears are for sadness, but some are for joy, Morgan. Sometimes I cry just thinking how hopeless things seemed to me when I was a child. Now I understand how my Mommo must've felt, losing her husband and living alone in a strange new country with four little children. I probably would've done the same thing if it had happened to me.*

I'm happy and grateful we're spending this time together. If we continue my story, we might be finished before it's time to carve the turkey. Are you girls ready to hear more?

"*Yes, please go on. I smell the turkey, but nobody's calling for us to come downstairs to the dining room yet,*" said Madison as she snuggled closer to BaBa, curling her hair around her pudgy little fingers.

Morgan left the room and quickly returned placing some pink tissues lovingly into her BaBa's lap. "*I'm ready,*" she said.

"*Okay, so let's continue.*"

The Homecoming

The long trip from America to Europe was painful and dangerous — painful because we traveled for weeks on a boat, a train and a wagon. The dangerous part was the train ride from Bratislava, a large city in Slovakia on the Danube River, to the city of Brezno.

A Slovak passenger warned Mommo that bandits had been robbing trains. If Mommo had any money, she needed to hide it fast! He said there were many robberies from the fall of 1918 to the spring of 1919. The war hadn't been over very long, and things hadn't settled down yet. European governments were very unstable. Times were hard. There was much poverty. People were doing whatever they had to do to feed themselves and their families. For some people, robbing trains was one way to get money.

Mommo nudged Mary to wake up. "Follow me to the toilet."

She needed to find a private place so she could hide our money. Mary followed her to the first class car. That's where the only toilet and lavatory were located on the train. Oh, what horrors it was every morning and evening when everyone needed to wait to use that one toilet!

They walked through a narrow passageway through the center of the first class car. Mommo pinned all the money she had in her bra, her pants and Mary's pants. When she returned, her face was flushed. It gave her a soft look that I wished she would've had all the time. Her flushed cheeks were caused from fear, not from the warm and crowded train. She worried that everything we owned could be stolen in minutes by robbers.

Before long, we heard the bandits had boarded the

first class car. They never came to our car. I guess they thought the passengers in our car were too poor and wouldn't have enough money to bother with. George was disappointed because he said he missed all the action.

Mommo said, "Hush up! You need to thank God our money is safe."

❧❧

I stared out the window for a long time. The farther the train moved from Bratislava, the more I missed Deddo and our home in America. The farther we traveled, the sadder I became leaving everything behind that I knew and loved.

The train was very dark and dingy. Smoke filled the air from the men smoking pipes and cigars. I could hardly breathe. I held on tightly to Mary for comfort. She kissed my cheek and rubbed my elbow. As I weeped softly in her ear, she said, "Don't cry, honey. We'll go back to America some day. You'll see."

I buried my face in her lap and soon cried myself to sleep.

When the train stopped in Brezno, I woke up and looked outside. It was early morning. It was so foggy and damp. I kept rubbing my eyes, hoping it would help me see more clearly. Outlines of the mountains in the distance towered up to the sky and disappeared into the fog. Everything was brushed a dreary brown and green. The sun was throwing bright red glows peeking behind the mountains.

I spotted an old man sitting on top of a rickety beat-up wagon that had chips of wood missing. He looked tall and had a long gray beard and bushy hair that fell below a black felt hat with a short round brim. He was dressed in a long cape trimmed in black piping with a vest underneath embroidered in red and green along the edges. His pants were a light material worn out at the knees, and he wore high black leather boots that must've been used for

18

many years. He looked like he was waiting for someone as he carefully watched each person climbing down the train steps from every car while smoking a long silver pipe. "What kind of mangy animal is pulling that wagon?" I asked Mary.

"That's a mule," she said.

As soon as Mommo looked at where I was pointing, she cried out, "That's your *Stary Otec* (Grandfather)! He's come to take us home."

Home? I thought, *this isn't my home.* I didn't know anything here and didn't even want to know anything here. My home was far away in America. I never wanted to leave.

Mommo's face lit up like the candles we put on our Christmas tree. I hadn't seen her so happy since Deddo called her "my sweetheart"...and that was a long, long time ago.

She couldn't get out of the train fast enough to run into her father's arms. They cried and held each other tightly for such a long time that I thought they'd never break apart. Mommo burrowed her head in his chest and kept telling him how happy she was to be in his arms again. My heart ached as I watched. I would never, ever again have a Deddo to hug me.

"Children, this is your grandfather. You can call him Otec." Mommo introduced each of us to him. She had always told us stories about her dad. She said he was the most lovable man in the family. His heart was as big as he was. No wonder she was happy to see him now that she didn't have a husband to hug anymore. She had said she would always go with him to town for trips to sell their vegetables and wood and bring home flour and other needed goods. He'd always save a few *haleru* (Slovak coins) to buy some candy treats for her. It was their secret. She'd hide the treats in her apron so her Momma wouldn't know. Her Momma said that Otec spoiled her. She said he was happiest when the gypsies visited the village and played their music, which he loved. He'd always stamp his feet and clap his hands to the music. You could always hear his singing while he worked in the fields.

He gave each of us a big hug and kiss as we gathered all our belongings and packed them onto the back of the wagon. They were our seats for the last part of our trip. He said if the mule was peppy this morning, we could probably get to Pohorelá, Mommo's village, in about an hour. But the dirt road was pretty wet from the spring rains, and the mule and wagon kept sinking into the mud.

"The family is waiting to celebrate your homecoming," said Otec, spouting out chunks of broken English while he talked. "We were sad to hear about Karl's death. When we get home, we'll tell you about all the changes since the war ended. Life has been pretty bad here. I'm not sure you made the right decision returning to Europe with the children. So much has gotten worse. Slovakia is not yet an independent country."

The countryside was beautiful. The mountains that got lost in the clouds weren't like anything we'd ever seen in Ohio. The sun was slowly burning off the fog. We got a better view of the hills and trees as the sun finally rose above the mountains, full of hope for a new brighter beginning.

Otec told us all about Pohorelá during the trip home. It was nestled in the middle of Slovakia, in the narrow valley of the river Hron between the steep walls of two chains of mountains: the Low Tatras and the Murans. He said the rugged Tatra Mountains spread across the central and northern parts of Slovakia. Pohorelá was a small farming village with a population of about twenty seven hundred. The biggest city of the region, Brezno, was a little less than two miles away. That's where PaPa and Otec traveled to buy supplies and sell their vegetables, wood and other goods.

"I'm hungry," interrupted George. "Is there anything to eat?"

Otec came prepared with some juicy pears that he handed to each of us.

As we approached Pohorelá, we passed an iron works factory that Otec said hadn't been doing well since the war ended. People in Mommo's village were farmers and not much interested in factory work.

As we arrived into the heart of the village, we saw rows of wooden log houses lined up across the dirt road from each other. A creek was located behind the houses. There were narrow wooden logs laid across the creek that connected the backs of one row of houses to the backs of another row of houses.

"All these small houses look exactly alike," said Mary. "How can you tell one from another? They sure look a lot different than the houses in Ohio."

As Otec turned onto the road between the houses, we saw Mommo's family outside, all happily waving at us and shouting, "Welcome, *Americankas.*" That's what everyone in the village would call us.

"Slovaks who live in America are considered to be successful, lucky and rich," explained Otec. "When you're called *Americankas*, it means people admire you because you lived in the land of opportunity and freedom. They'll have a hard time understanding why you wanted to leave to come here, where we're suffering from poverty, hunger, fighting, hard work and being controlled by other people and governments."

It took the family a long time to help us unload the wagon because of all the hugging, chattering and crying with joy. Every single one of them pinched my cheeks and hugged me so hard that I felt like a pin cushion, or an accordion that had squeezed out too many songs.

We all gathered into Otec's house for a family meeting. Mommo started off introducing the youngest to the family. "This is my baby, Julia. She looks so much like Mary. They both have beautiful auburn hair. She's very quiet, shy and small for a two year old. You all remember Mary and George. You see that George, who is nine, looks just like his Deddo. I think he'll be tall like him." Mommo had to fight back her tears while looking at George, because she was seeing her Karl.

"George is also lazy and spoiled. Otec, maybe you can put him to work in the fields," laughed Mary.

"Oh, I think there's enough work for all of us. No one's spoiled here," said Otec. It didn't take long for us to realize how true those words were.

"And my outspoken oldest daughter, Mary, is twelve. She's talkative, bold and takes care of her sisters and brother for me.

"Last is Anna. I call her *ciganocka* (my little gypsy) because she likes pretty, colorful clothes. I think she'll like the Slovak dress with all its fancy embroidery and colors. She's now four, tall, skinny and sickly. She used to sing a lot and was happy like her Deddo, until he died. Now she's been sad ever since we left America. She's allergic to milk and has a bad stomach. She had the flu the same time as Karl. I don't know how God took my Karl, who was healthy, and left Anna, who was sickly. She's always been so frail. We never thought she'd live much beyond three years old, but here she is." Mommo never looked at me the whole time during my introduction.

My heart sank. Again, I felt those words stabbing me. I guess Mommo will never change. She'll never let me forget that somehow God had sacrificed Deddo for me. Otec walked over to me and hugged me tightly.

He interrupted Mommo in mid-sentence: "Maria, don't say that," he scolded. "We don't know why things happen as they do. You shouldn't make Anna feel guilty she's alive."

Mommo turned her head to show she didn't acknowledge his interruption or his reprimand.

From that moment on, Otec and I became very close. He felt my sorrow. Mommo never said that again to me as long as he was close enough to hear her.

Mommo began to introduce her family to us. "Children, this is your *Stara Mat* (grandmother). You can call her Stara."

Stara had salt and pepper hair which must have been very long. She had it braided and fastened on the back of her head like a big round pinwheel. She had rosy cheeks, a twinkle in her eyes and looked just like Mommo except for a few more wrinkles and a rounded back that I realized must've been caused from lots of hard work in the fields.

By the time we were introduced to our Great-Grandparents, NaNa and PaPa, Julia and I were already warmly cuddled in their laps looking over their strange clothes. They each had colorful vests that reached to their waists. PaPa was dressed like Otec with boots, pants and an embroidered shirt. NaNa had a long, narrow white apron that hung from her waist to the bottom of her skirt. Her blouse had puffy sleeves that came to her elbows and a floppy collar edged in red embroidery. She had a faded cloth cover tied around her head.

Lastly, there were *Stryna* (Aunt) Ann, who I was named after and *Stryk* (Uncle) John. They lived across the road. Stryna was Mommo's sister, and they had a baby named Johnny. Later that day, other family members came to meet us. All in all, there were about twenty more including lots of cousins.

The family decided that Mary, Julia and I would stay with our Grandparents and NaNa and PaPa. We were pretty happy about that. The three of us always took care of each other. We would sleep together in one bed in this strange new house. Mommo and George would live with Stryna Ann, Stryk John and Johnny.

23

Both houses were exactly alike inside. They each had a long, wooden table with chairs and benches and a fireplace in a large gathering room where all activities occurred. There was a large, white ceramic oven that helped heat the house while cooking the meals. That large oven would be my favorite place. I would sit on the oven ledge to keep warm during the bitter cold winters. There were two bare windows that looked onto the side of the house. There were two small rooms for sleeping. A well, an outhouse, a smokehouse, a hen house and a barn were all located in the back by the creek.

We ate a dinner of delicious bread baked by NaNa, sausage, dumplings, and potato balls rolled in sauerkraut. Now it was time to be educated in the conditions of Pohorelá and Slovakia during and after the war. Otec did most of the talking.

"During the war, Maria, there was no fighting in Slovakia. Many Slovaks were sent to fight in Piava in northern Italy and to Zborov in Russia. Many were killed and wounded. After the war ended on October 28, 1918, Slovakia did not have its own government. It only had geographic, cultural, and ethical borders. Slovakia still has not become an independent country, but has been created within Czecho-Slovakia on the ruins of the Austro-Hungarian Empire. The Magyars troops invaded us. They took over some parts of southern and eastern Czechoslovakia until just this past spring, 1919.[6] You are lucky to come back after all this."

"We've seen many fights within our territory since you left. The Czechs, who outnumber us, are very different from us. We're mainly farmers and they are not. We're mainly Catholic and they are not. Czech leadership now is trying to limit the power of our church. We're less educated than they are, and have less experience governing ourselves. Government control is located in the capital city of Prague, which is on the Czech side."[7]

"We're very unhappy with this new state. First we were dominated by the Magyars. Now we're dominated by the Czechs. Tensions between the Slovaks and Czechs continue to heat up. The attitude of the Czechs to the Slovaks is described by words in their encyclopedia. It describes Slovakia as a 'Czech colony.' We have yet to become independent with our own political government."

"How's the money situation now with this new partnership?" asked Mommo.

"Much of the poverty we're all suffering from is due to having to pay for the war that caused so many to die or be wounded. There are many pensions paid to the wounded and to the relatives of the dead. We're also paying to restore the areas destroyed by the war. The war was very expensive. Most of the men were called to serve in the army. There was nobody to make money except old people and women. So, you see, Maria, this is a bad time for us. To make matters worse, most of Europe hasn't recovered from the war and now we're being threatened by the increasing strength of communists in Russia.[8] We don't know what's going to happen with them. Our farm barely produces enough food for all of us. We hear if they occupy our land, they'll take most of what we grow and produce. I can see that you, George and Mary will give us six more hands to help in the fields."

"But, I don't know how to farm," implored George. He was hoping to be excused from working in the fields with everyone else.

"That's okay, you look strong. You'll be a fast learner, and in no time we'll turn you into a first-class farmer," laughed Otec.

That's not what George wanted to hear, and looking very disappointed, he dropped his head and shook it from left to right as if to say, *that's not going to work for me.*

"Well, we're here now. We need to make the best of it," said Mommo. "We'll do everything we can to help out.

I brought some money that can help us. After Karl died, I didn't know what to do or how to take care of *moje sirotky*, or myself. I just had to return home! You know I never really wanted to go to America anyway. It was Karl's dream and now he's gone. After Karl died, I was angry at him, angry at God, angry at Anna and angry at myself. I needed to come back home."

"I understand. We'll do our best to make this work, Maria. We love you and the children. I just hope that you'll not live to regret leaving America."

Life in Czechoslovakia

The cold, rugged winters were long and lasted from the end of October until the end of March. The soil was barren. These were poor conditions for people who spent their lives farming. The only major crops grown that kept the village people fed were potatoes, onions and cabbage. All meals used a combination of them with flour, bread and meat, which didn't provide much variety. Life was hard in this new land. Pasturage, woodcutting and wood trading were more developed than farming.

Everyone except NaNa, PaPa, Julia and I worked in the fields from dawn to dusk. Mommo, Mary and George soon became skilled at farming. George continued to complain bitterly that he hated farming. He was even getting calluses on his hands. Otec said, "When your calluses get as big as mine, then you become a real farmer!"

George said, "No, thank you!"

Barns in Pohorelá courtesy of Dr. Lubor Matejko, Comenius
University in Slovak Republic

Julia and I were too young to work in the fields. We had other jobs to help the family. I took care of Julia and baby Johnny, fed the chickens and pigs, gathered eggs and picked apples and pears from the trees when they were ripe enough to eat. Julia set the table every evening for dinner. Julia and I liked the apples NaNa soaked in sauerkraut juice. They were our treat.

PaPa took care of the animals and cured the meat in the smokehouse. Our first summer there was blazing hot and the following winter was freezing cold. Sometimes when the cold rolled in, the ceramic oven and fireplace couldn't keep ice from forming on the walls of the house and windows. I think I spent most of that first winter perched atop the oven whenever I wasn't busy with chores.

George and Mary started school that fall. Mary was so pretty that many boys wanted to walk her home from school. One day when one of the boys walked her home, he threw his arms around her and kissed her. She said she didn't kiss him back. She was shocked, but enjoyed all the attention from the boys. Mommo shook her finger and hollered, "You better not get sweet on any boys. We may be going back to America some day!"

That was the first time I ever heard her hint that she had any thoughts of returning home since it hadn't even been a year since we left.

Every Sunday, the church bells rang throughout the village. Everyone gathered to pray together. I always snuggled myself between Mary and NaNa. I loved to watch NaNa pray with the beautiful brown and white wooden rosaries PaPa carved for her. I watched her gnarly, bony fingers roll over each wooden bead of the rosary as she silently prayed, mouthing the words throughout the mass. Sunday was the day we could all be together, sing with our neighbors and catch up on all the village gossip.

We were the center of attention for weeks after we

arrived. People made us feel like celebrities. They wanted to know about the *Americankas*. They were hungry to hear what life was like in this country where everyone was free to do and say and buy whatever they wanted.

Following mass one Sunday, cousin Helen took Mommo aside as we were walking home. She began crying. "Maria, you remember Joe, my husband. They put him in the army and sent him to Italy to fight in the war. He was killed by a German sniper. Just like you, I'm alone with four children to care for. It rained a lot last summer and we didn't have much of a harvest. The children and I suffered through a long winter without much food. I don't know what I'm going to do to keep things going. Could you help me?"

Mommo and Helen cried all the way home. "I know how you feel. I miss my Karl too. If you stop by the house later, I have some money to help you until the spring planting and harvest."

As we finished dinner later that day, Otec lingered at the table drinking his coffee. He asked Mommo to join him. She sat down. For a long time, he didn't say a word. She just sat quietly waiting until he was ready to speak. Finally, he put his cup down and began his warning. "Maria, I told you there's much poverty in this village. You're going to hear many sad stories. You can't feel sorry for everyone. If you don't think of your children first, your money will be gone before you know it! Everyone just thinks *Americankas* have lots of money. They think their streets are lined with gold, but you know and I know that's not true. I know you feel sorry for Helen. Mark my words, as soon as you give her money, more friends and family will be looking for handouts."

"I've been writing to Karl's Aunt Katie in America. If I need more money, I know she'll help us," Mommo replied with an attitude letting him know she was not willing to listen. She stood up and brushed past Otec, clearing

People from Pohorelá

the dishes with her head held high in the air. She didn't like to be told what to do.

But Otec was right. It wasn't long before she was approached by others for help. She continued to give friends and family money. Soon, she realized her money was running low. Aunt Katie wrote that she wouldn't be able to send her any money because times were also tough in Ohio.

Our first hard winter was so long we knew our food supply wouldn't last long. Otec had to go into town to sell two of our pigs to buy enough food to keep us fed until spring. But spring brought so much rain that there was no bumper crop of vegetables to sell in town, nor even to keep us fed. I realized then how farmers' lives depended totally on the weather.

The longer we were in Europe, the less happy Mommo seemed. I even overheard her tell Stara that she was beginning to miss America. I was shocked! Was there anything that would make her happy again? Mary told me I worried too much for a little girl and that's probably why my stomach was always upset.

As we lay in our bed one night, Julia and I eavesdropped on NaNa and PaPa's conversation. "I'm worried about Maria,"said NaNa. "She's foolishly given away most of her money even though she was warned. I know she's not happy being here. She showers all her attention on George and Mary, and doesn't spend any time with the little ones. She told Stara she never should've left America, and that things are so bad here, she needs to make plans to go back."

"She also told me that if she ever wanted to return to America, she would have to make arrangements soon," said PaPa. "The government papers permitting her to come to Europe were only good for a limited time. If she wants to leave, it would have to be soon since she and George and Mary aren't American citizens. Time is running out for them."

"Julia," I whispered, "do you think we'll actually be going home soon? Just think, maybe Mommo is finally changing. I'm so happy. Soon, we'll be back in America."

Goodbye, Mommo

Mommo called a family meeting one evening. I was chasing Julia around the oven while everyone was finishing their meal.

"Anna, you and Julia must stop playing and sit down with us," she said.

I noticed her lip quivering. Her voice cracked as if she didn't know if any more words would come out. Julia quickly jumped on PaPa's lap and I on NaNa's. It took a long time before she was able to continue. "I have something I need to tell all of you," she said. "We've been here for several months. The children and I are so grateful you welcomed us during these tough times. We've tried to help out and make it work, but I've decided we need to return to America before it's too late."

"What does that mean, before it's too late?" questioned Stryna Ann.

"The visa that allowed us to travel to Europe will soon expire. I still have some money left to buy our tickets, but I don't have enough money to buy tickets for all of us."

"Who's all of us?" questioned Mary.

Now Mommo's voice wasn't only cracking, but it also was so low Otec asked her to speak up. Everyone was so quiet, even Julia and I, that you could hear the wind whistling through the trees outside.

With her head down and not looking at anyone, she continued. "As you know, Anna and Julia are American citizens because they were born there, but George, Mary and I are not. If the three of us don't leave before our visa expires, we might never be able to return." She was wringing her hands so tightly around her apron that they were as white as PaPa's hair. "So, if I have your blessing, I'll be taking Mary and George with me to America. I'm asking if Anna and Julia could stay a while longer with you until I make enough money to send for them later."

Before she had enough time to finish her sentence, I jumped off NaNa's lap and ran over to her. I grabbed her hands, looked directly into her eyes and screamed, "You can't take Mary away from me!" I was so scared to be defying her, I could barely talk. I never did that before. "No! No! I won't let you take Mary away from me!" I could hardly see for the tears streaming from my eyes like two faucets. I ran to Mary and held onto her skirt. She kissed my cheek and rubbed my elbow, only this time it didn't work. I didn't feel any better. I knew I couldn't live without her. Now Julia started crying. Then Mary started choking back tears. "Mary, did you know about this?" I cried.

She sadly shook her head, no.

"Anna, sit down and be quiet," said Mommo. It won't be forever. As soon as we get back to America and save enough money, we'll send for you and Julia. You're getting everyone all upset. We'll be staying with cousin Katie. There is a lot of work there, and before long, we'll all be together again."

"How long do you think it'll be?" asked Stryna Ann. "You know my baby will be here in a few months."

I can't make any promises with time. Anna will be able to help you when the baby comes. She's been taking care of Julia ever since she was born."

"You won't send for us," I cried out. "You're still mad that I didn't die. You're happy you can finally leave me behind. And now you're even taking Mary away from me, too."

"This is not about you, Anna," said Mommo, "I have..."

Otec interrupted her. "We want to help you, Maria, but have you thought everything through? You were quick to leave America when Karl died and now you're making another quick decision to return." The air was tense. No one moved or dared speak. Otec talked calmly. "Maybe you need to give this some more thought. These are big decisions for you and the children. Remember, these two little ones lost their father and now they'll be losing their mother. Have you thought about that?"

"Yes, I have, but I don't have much time left. They're not losing me. This is the best I can do right now. I can't risk not being able to return to America. We've been a burden on all of you. I know it's been hard having to feed five extra mouths. I had no idea how much suffering you've all endured since I left years ago with Karl. I was only thinking about my own grief. I'm sorry, but we need to go back to America before it's too late.

"How soon do you think you'll be leaving?" asked Stara.

"We need to be gone within the month. PaPa, if you take me into town tomorrow, I can check on all the arrangements."

Mary started humming in my ear. She was trying to be brave, but I could feel her warm tears trickling onto my cheek. Her hands were cold and clammy. I couldn't get my body to stop shaking. My stomach was tied in knots. I knew I wouldn't be able to live without her.

From that day on whenever Mommo and I brushed past each other, there were never any words spoken or eye contact. It's as if I was invisible to her.

I finally broke our silence to ask an important question the day they were preparing to leave. "Can I pleaaasssse take the wagon ride into Brezno with you?" I begged.

"It's better if you stay home with NaNa," she said without feeling, not looking at me as she answered.

As everyone was packing the wagon and preparing to leave, Mary found me in the bedroom. She handed me

34

the rag doll NaNa made for her. "Whenever you get scared and lonely, I want you to close your eyes and squeeze my doll. I'll be able to feel you squeezing me in my heart all the way to Ohio."

"Really?" I cried, as I cuddled her doll to my chest.

"Yes, really," she answered. "Anna, you and I have a golden thread that attaches to both of us. It connects your heart to my heart and it doesn't make any difference how far or close we are to each other. We'll always be attached. When you squeeze my doll, I'll feel it in my heart. I'll write to you as much as I can and I promise on Deddo's grave that we'll send for you and Julia as soon as we can. I'll keep after Mommo until you're with us again. I promise you. Do you believe me?"

She waited for my response. I nodded. "You know I believe you more than anyone else in the world."

PaPa and Otec loaded up the wagon. When it was time to leave, Mary and George were saying their final good-byes to everyone and ready to board the wagon.

Anna," Mary called out as she looked around for me.

There was no answer. Mary called out, "Anna",

Mother with kids from Pohorelá in festive attire

35

again. "Anna!" she yelled. George dropped his bag and began to help Mary search for me. They looked in every corner, in the barn, the smokehouse and even inside the outhouse.

"Anna's gone. Where can she be?" Mary asked the others worriedly. "She's not the type to run off."

"Where can she be indeed!" said a voice behind them.

George and Mary turned around. Mommo was standing in the doorway watching as they searched for Anna. Her eyes were stern and impatient. "Let's go, or we'll miss the train!"

NaNa stopped Mommo in her tracks. "You can't leave without saying goodbye to her! Her heart is broken enough as it is. Just wait here. She can't be too far. Mary and I will find her."

They looked around the scraggly yard in front and behind the house. Mary spotted the colored ribbon in Anna's hair peaking just above the bucket hanging from the well. Mary had an odd feeling in her stomach as she and NaNa walked over to where I was crouched over, hiding my face between my knees behind the well. They put their arms around my shoulders and lifted me to my feet.

"Anna, I promise you I won't let Mommo rest a day until we bring you and Julia home with us. We'll never be a family until we're all together again. Do you believe me?" she asked as she stared deep into my eyes.

I didn't respond. NaNa stroked my hair as we all walked to the wagon where everyone was waiting.

I kissed George. I put my head down as I walked over to Mommo, and barely touched her cheek with my lips. She was in no mood for any loving goodbyes. I saved the last kiss and bear hug for Mary. My legs could barely carry me to her side. "What am I going to do without you?" I sobbed.

"What did I tell you to do when you're lonely and scared?" she asked.

"I know," I whispered.

"Well, then tell me."

"I'll just squeeze your doll", I whimpered.

"That's right. We'll always be together no matter what!" she reminded me.

I held onto NaNa and Mary's doll as the wagon pulled away. We watched them until they were out of sight. I really believed Mary about the doll, and it was with me wherever I went.

After all, I could always count on Mary like the sun coming up every morning and setting every evening. She loved me more than anyone else in the whole wide world.

That night I had a dream for the first time that would repeat over and over and over again for the rest of my life.

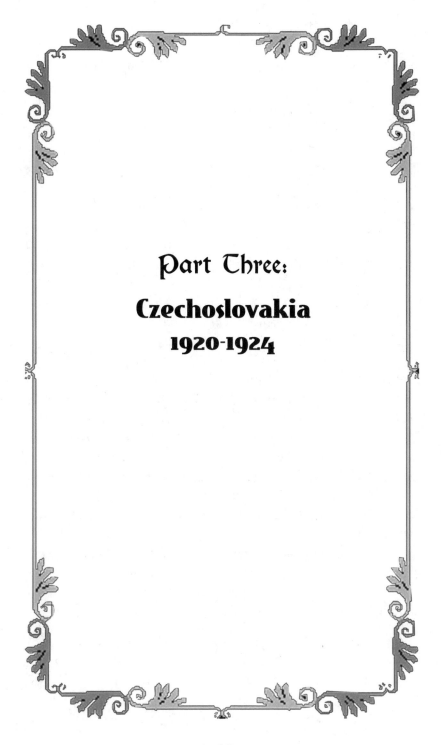

Part Three:

Czechoslovakia

1920-1924

"Well, don't stop there, BaBa. Tell us your dream again before you continue the story," whispered Morgan.

"Before I do, does anyone think the turkey might be done?" asked BaBa.

"Wait here," said Madison. "I'll run downstairs and see if dinner's ready."

Before BaBa could answer, she was gone and in a flash, she was back.

"Daddy said dinner would be ready in another hour. Will you be able to finish your story by then?" asked Madison.

"I think I can."

"Well, don't forget to tell us about your dream first," said Morgan. "I want to hear it again. I have lots of dreams, but they're all different. They're never the same."

BaBa continued, "I'm always lost in my dream. I have no shoes on and yet I'm running. I don't know where I'm going. I see lots of people in my dream, but I don't know any of them. I see Deddo, but I can't seem to reach him. I see his face everywhere I look: in the fields, in town, and even at the bottom of a well. NaNa said my dream means I'm feeling lost and abandoned because I was left behind in Europe. Seeing Deddo and not being able to reach him means it's not my time to be with him in heaven."

"I'm glad it's not your time to be in heaven, BaBa. If it was, Madison and I wouldn't be able to visit you every year, hear your story and hug and kiss you," cried Morgan, as she snuggled so close to BaBa she was almost on her lap.

"And I wouldn't even have two Great-Grand-daughters growing up to be such beautiful fourth generation Americans! Now let's all dry our tears together and go on before that turkey's ready to carve."

Missing Mary

The days were long after Mary left. NaNa said she never heard me sing anymore and that my smiling face must've left with Mary. She tried to cheer me up, but it didn't help. Nothing could, short of reuniting with my family. Mary's rag doll was always with me. I would squeeze it, hoping that somehow I could feel Mary squeezing me back. I kept having that dream about being barefoot and trying to reach Deddo.

"Anna, stop moping around here. Your sadness is rubbing off on Julia and you're making her sad too. If you and Julia would fill your time with other things, before you know it you'll be on your way back to America. You better start eating, or you'll be too sick and skinny to make the trip back. The best way to forget about your unhappiness is to give to others who need you. Take a special interest in some of the farm animals."

I took NaNa's advice and picked out one of the pigs as my pet and named her Pinky. She had a steady eye and always followed closely behind my heels whenever I was in the pen feeding her and the other pigs. I named a chicken, Feathers, and spoiled her with special treats. NaNa promised me we would never eat Feathers as long as I lived there.

One hot afternoon while everyone was working in the fields, PaPa yelled, "Anna, Anna, hurry and come quickly to the barn. I need your help!"

As I reached the barn, I spotted one of our cows half lying on the ground and half trying to get to her feet. "What's the matter with the cow, PaPa?"

"Anna, hold the cow's head on the ground and try to calm her down. She's almost ready to give birth to her calf. The more you calm her, the easier will be her delivery."

That was my first experience learning the mysteries of birth and life. I knew about the end of life when Deddo died. I knew Stryna Ann was going to have a baby soon, but it wasn't until I helped PaPa with the birth of the calf that I began to understand the beginning of life.

I held the cow's head in my arms while she thrashed around, moaning a funny sound I never heard before. I could tell she was in pain. PaPa finally delivered a beautiful brown and white spotted calf. As soon as she entered the world, she wobbled to a standing position on her skinny wet legs. She looked so helpless, I called her "Baby". Baby soon began to nurse with her mommy. Julia was disappointed that she missed the whole thing while she was taking her afternoon nap.

Until Stryna Ann's baby was born, I spent most of my time playing and taking care of Julia, Baby, Feathers and Pinky. NaNa was right. Taking special care of my pets did help take my homesickness away. It gave me something else to think about besides my unhappiness. It was at bedtime that I would think of Mary and my sadness would return.

NaNa added some chores now that I was getting older and more responsible. She showed me how to remove fur from the sheep to make yarn and thread, and I also began to help prepare the meals. We started to crochet a beautiful yellow, green and white shawl together. The colors reminded me of a meadow with colorful flowers. She said I could take it back to America with me when it was finished. The shawl was a special project we worked on every evening after dinner by candlelight.

I would watch NaNa's wrinkled arthritic fingers in the candlelight flying through each stitch. I loved to watch her crochet every stitch lovingly into that shawl. I knew I'd never forget the peaceful evenings we enjoyed working together.

"I'll bet you could do that in the dark with your eyes closed," I giggled.

"You bet I could, and pretty soon you'll be able to do it too," she said.

NaNa had such a small face and hunched over body, it was difficult to imagine that this tiny woman was able to work as hard as she did, day in and day out: baking bread every day, cooking the meals, bringing buckets of water in from the well. There was no rest for any of us except on Sundays, but even then, many things required work.

PaPa had a wheel in the barn where he sharpened his knives. Julia and I would join him, playing in the large haystack piled high against the barn. Over and over we would climb up the haystack and jump down, giggling all the way. Then we'd pick straw out of each other's hair. It was probably the only fun we ever had while we lived there, and it didn't happen very often.

In Pohorelá, children worked as hard as everyone else. There was never any time for fun.

It was months before we received the first letter from Mommo. She said they were all getting settled with jobs. She sent some money to take care of Julia and me. Inside the letter was a note for me from Mary. I waited until that evening when NaNa and I were preparing to crochet to have her read it to me. I sat on her lap, holding my doll.

My sweet Anna,

The trip took so long that I thought we would never get to Ohio. George is cleaning a general store around the corner from Aunt Katie's house. I'm watching three children next door and helping their mother cook and clean. We're all earning money. We have six Slovak men tenants living in the house. They all work different shifts in a factory. They sleep in three beds. When the men are at work during the day, the men that worked at night are home sleeping. And when the men are at work during the night, the men that worked during the day are home sleeping. Aunt Katie calls them her boarders. They pay us lots of money.

Mommo and Aunt Katie keep the house and cook for all of us. So, you see my dear Anna, we're all saving money to bring you and Julia back as soon as we can.

I've felt you often in my heart. I know you must be squeezing my doll a lot. Put my letter under your pillow so you could hear me talk to you in my prayers. Don't cry too much. Give Julia a big hug and kiss for me and tell her I love her.

Love,
Mary

Inside the note were two pieces of gum for Julia and me. With the money Mommo sent, PaPa said we would ride into town to buy some boots and clothes. NaNa said it was high time I prepare for school since I would be turning seven real soon.

The short ride to town was fun. PaPa taught me one of his songs.

> *Work, work, that's our life.*
> *One fine day when my work is done,*
> *I'm going to fly away home.*
> *I'm going to fly away home.*

He even let me hold the reins and drive the wagon. When we got to the store to buy my boots, I spotted a silver and red harmonica. I picked it up and began blowing into it.

44

"Anna, put that down! We didn't come to buy you any harmonica. There's no money for such foolishness."

"Please, can I have it, PaPa?"

"No, now stop crying and put it down! Wait for me in the wagon."

I don't remember PaPa being so stern with me before. I waited in the wagon while he finished selling our vegetables, fruit and wood. Then he called me back into the store. He bought me a pair of shiny black leather boots that were so big they flopped around on my feet. PaPa said they had to last me a long time and I'd grow into them. We had enough money left over for a dress, skirt and heavy wool coat.

On the trip home, I was very quiet and so was he. I broke the silence and asked, "PaPa, are you mad at me about the harmonica? Is that why you're not talking?"

"No, honey. I'm mad because of other things." With that, he pulled a newspaper from under his coat. "This had nothing to do with you. I'm disgusted with what I'm reading in the newspaper. It's all about what's happening to our people with our new country, Czechoslovakia. You heard me telling your Mommo about the partnership our people made with the Czechs so we could finally be independent. We thought it would be the end of being controlled by other people. That never happened. Now the Czechs continue to control us. They want us to be factory workers instead of farmers. Well, we don't want to work in their factories. This new government isn't what we want. I'm just angry that things never seem to change in our favor. All the best jobs in state administration — railroads, post offices, schools — are going to the Czechs, not to us. It seems we'll never be able to improve our lives. That's why I'm angry. It had nothing to do with you, honey."

PaPa lifted me onto his lap and together we held the reins and drove the wagon singing our song over and over.

45

We ate the bread, eggs and apples NaNa packed for our trip. When we finished, he said, "Open your apron, Anna."

He slipped four red hard candy squares into the pocket of my apron. He had a big smile and put his finger to his mouth as if to say, it's our secret. I ate two squares that tasted sweeter than anything I had ever eaten. I put them in my mouth one by one. I didn't chew them. I just let them slowly melt so they would last longer. I saved the other two for Julia. We never told NaNa about our treats.

After Julia and I went to bed, we heard PaPa, Otec and Stryk John talking about how lucky Mommo was to get back to America. Stryk John said he wanted to leave and move his family to America too, and maybe Mommo could help him. Otec said he would send Mommo a letter explaining John's wish.

That fall I started school for the first time. I walked with friends every day to our one room, log schoolhouse. There were about twenty children of all ages in that one room. We were separated by age.

There were two large wooden tables and four benches. Nails were along one wall near the door where we hung our coats and hats. If our boots were too small and our feet hurt, we were allowed to take them off and line them up under our coats. There was no snow removal in the winter. If the snow was piled too high for us to walk through, school would close for the day.

Our subjects were reading, writing, arithmetic and singing songs. The subjects were different for different age groups, but we all had the same teacher. He wanted to be called Professor. His name was Jozef, but we called him 'Mean Man' behind his back. We were scared of him. He had a black patch over his eye, and was tall and dark. He looked like the character Ichabod Crane in the story *Legend of Sleepy Hollow*. He had a switch that he used to hit us on the back of our hands whenever we laughed, misbehaved or did anything he believed to be annoying. He had no sense of humor. He wouldn't even let me keep my rag doll at school.

"There's no place for dolls in school, *Americanka*," he scoffed as he hit my doll with his switch. "From now on, leave it at home!"

The evil look on his face when he called me *Americanka* made me think there was something wrong with me because I was an American.

"I need to have my doll with me," I said. "I get sick when she's not with me."

"Too bad your doll doesn't help you learn. I won't permit it!" He swatted me over the back of my hands. Red marks popped up on my knuckles. Mary's doll never came to school with me again.

NaNa tied my lunch in a cotton napkin. She usually packed an apple, bread with butter and a piece of bacon. We ate our lunches at our table. In the winter, the professor let us eat our lunch huddled around the wood stove to keep warm.

I wore the boots PaPa bought for me for three long years. My feet were growing, but the boots weren't. I would take them off as soon as I got to school. I wrapped rags around my feet to keep warm. It was painful wearing those boots walking to and from school and church. The most pleasure I had during those years was taking them off as soon as I got home and rubbing my feet. PaPa said he couldn't afford to buy me new boots until Mommo sends him more money.

School began at the end of harvest season and lasted until planting season. I never worked in the fields like some of my friends. When school was over, I took care of Stryna Ann's little boy, Johnny. Within a short time, Johnny had a baby sister, Veronica. We called her Vernie. I took care of them as well as Julia. Taking care of the new baby almost brought an end to my life.

47

The Snake

We continued to receive letters from Mommo and Mary. News was always the same. They told us about their jobs and life with the boarders. Sometimes money was enclosed and sometimes not. She never mentioned how soon she would be sending for us, or that she even missed us. Mary always put two sticks of gum in the envelope. She said she prayed every night we would be coming home soon. She said she always felt a tug in her heart every time I squeezed her doll. Weeks turned into months and months into years.

The summer was hot and we had no rain. Everyone worried the well would run dry, the crops would burn up and we wouldn't have anything to sell in town to see us through the winter. Looking at the beautiful Tatras, we could see snow on the tallest mountains and wished it would melt down to the village. We worried we'd be unable to water the fields and the animals.

I woke NaNa up one night when I heard lightning firing up in the sky. With each hit, there were beautiful designs flashing on and off, lighting up our house like it was in the middle of the day. It lasted half the night. You could almost smell that the rain was hanging above the clouds ready to pour down, but it never did.

I ran to her bed. "NaNa, it's finally going to rain. Look outside at the lightning and listen to the loud thunder."

"It's only heat lightning, honey. It doesn't mean the rain is coming. And why are you crying? What's wrong? You've never been scared of lightning before."

NaNa saw that my eyes were red, but it wasn't from

the lightning that made me cry. She lit a candle and sat up in bed. By this time, Julia was awake.

"I miss my family. I know I'll never see them again. Mommo never says anything in her letters about sending for us. She doesn't even say she misses us. Mary's the only one that keeps promising she wants us back."

Of course your Mommo wants you back. She's just trying to get settled and earn enough money. You need to have faith that someday soon, you'll be going back home."

"Why doesn't she say anything about it then?" I asked.

"Maybe she's just as sad as you are. Maybe she's missing you so much, it's too painful for her to talk about it. I'm sure she feels bad that she can't get you back as quickly as she'd like. Did you ever think of that?"

"I don't think so. Mommo's still mad that I'm alive and Deddo's dead."

"Stop that, Anna. Your Mommo loves you just as much as she loves Julia, George and Mary. She might have said some harsh words to you a long time ago, but people do change."

I let NaNa talk, but I knew in my heart Julia and I would never leave Pohorelá. I tossed and turned that night, squeezing my doll and hoping Mary could feel it in her heart. NaNa was right. It didn't rain that night, but later that week, the storms finally came and some of the crops were saved.

My days were filled with caring for the new baby, Vernie. She loved when I rocked her in the little cloth hammock PaPa set up for us in the yard. Everyday after Stryna Ann finished nursing the baby, she would head out to the fields to join Stryk. I would take care of her until they returned.

One sunny morning while I was reading a book and rocking Vernie in the hammock, I heard some rustling in the grass below my boots. As I looked up from my book,

50

I spotted a long skinny brown snake crawling slowly up the rope that held the hammock to the tree. It was crawling towards Vernie's face. I was deathly afraid of snakes. We had lots of them in our village, especially in the bushes where the sweetest berries grew. I never went anywhere near those bushes. PaPa always warned me not to run if I saw any of them. "You'll only scare the snakes and then they jump half their size to bite you."

My instincts wouldn't let me be still with that ugly snake crawling closer and closer to Vernie. I jumped up like a frightened grasshopper and tried to shoo the snake away with my book. It leaped at me. As I screamed, "PaPa! PaPa! Help! A snake!" I felt a sting and throbbing pain on my left leg like being hit by a burning iron. I screamed so loud that the baby started crying. The whole village heard my blood curdling scream, "Ahhhhhhhhhh!"

PaPa was only about ten feet away from me. He jumped over the hammock and killed the snake with his shovel. He pulled out his knife, cut into my leg where the snake bit me and began to suck out the venom and blood. The pain in my leg was like hot metal burning right through me. It throbbed and stung. It began to swell like a balloon blowing up right before my eyes.

NaNa ran from the house and grabbed Vernie out of the hammock. She watched PaPa continue to suck the blood from my leg. When he finished, she wrapped a cloth tightly around my leg which had swelled double its size by now.

"I'm taking Anna to the doctor in town," said PaPa.

I don't even remember riding into Brezno. I was perspiring so much my clothes were sopping wet. Even my doll's dress was soaked. It was like the time I had the flu and Mary kept putting cold wet cloths on my head to bring down the fever. Only this time there was no Mary. There was no Mommo. PaPa said I was delirious and even scared him because I was talking funny.

I woke up hearing PaPa and the doctor talking.

"What kind of treatment does she need?" PaPa asked.

"I have cleaned it out as much as I can. There's not much else you can do now but pray that her leg doesn't swell anymore. If she gets an infection that prevents any healing, we'll need to amputate her leg. Where are her parents?"

"Her mother's in America and her father died a few years ago."

"Well, if we have to amputate, we'll need her mother's permission. I suggest you contact her immediately and get the necessary consent; otherwise, I can't help her anymore."

What did he mean, amputate my leg? How would I get along with only one leg? For sure, Mommo wouldn't want me. What more could possibly happen to me that hadn't already? All I could think about was I needed Mary, so I just held onto my doll and buried my tear-streaked face in her wet dress. The skin on my leg was stretched so much that any time I moved the least little bit, sharp pain shot through my leg, down my foot and into my back. The trip back to Pohorelá on the wagon seemed to take forever.

"PaPa, please go slow. Every bump makes me hurt more," I pleaded.

Everyone was waiting for us when we got back.

"Anna, you're a hero. You saved Vernie from the snake. She's so little, she would've died from the bite," said Stryna and Stryk. "Thank you, thank you."

"What's the doctor going to do for Anna?" asked NaNa as she removed the bandage to examine my leg.

"The doctor said if her leg swells anymore and she gets an infection, he'll have to cut it off…but before he can, we'll need to get Maria's permission for him to do it."

"Nobody is going to cut off my Great-Granddaughter's leg! I'll take care of her myself. And on my mother's grave, I promise that I'll not leave this earth until Anna's all healed and able to walk again!"

Hearing the words, 'cut off her leg,' terrified me more than ever. NaNa was true to her word. She might have been a small woman, but boy was she strong. She was determined she could nurse me back to health. I did get an infection. She applied hot horse manure compresses directly on the wound to draw out the infection. Did that ever stink! My leg hurt from the moment she applied the compresses until the moment she finished. Since I couldn't walk, PaPa put some wheels on a chair so I could scoot around when there was no one to carry me from place to place.

For six months, NaNa cared for me day and night. "Don't worry," she would say. "You're in my hands now. You'll walk and I'll be alive to see it."

I wasn't able to go to school that fall. I sure didn't miss being with that mean professor anyway.

A few months later, we received a letter from Mommo. She said she met a nice Slovak man named John, who had two children. They were planning to marry and maybe there would be enough money saved to send for us sooner than she thought.

"I won't be able to leave if I can't walk by the time Mommo sends money for the trip home. Her new husband won't want a cripple to take care of, will he?" I asked.

"You worry too much, *moje anjel*," she said. "Don't you believe I'll have you walking in time for you to make the trip?"

It was a long summer being confined to a chair with wheels and not being able to do much. There was no Indian Summer, and Fall came quickly with cold weather to follow. The cold weather didn't help NaNa. She coughed a lot, and it seemed her health slowly began to get worse. I don't know what it was because she was getting so old, or her devotion to taking care of me every day was making her sick. Stara had to take over cooking the meals for the family. NaNa spent all her time caring for me. She still applied those hot compresses several times a day until the swelling finally began to go down. She said it was time to begin putting some weight on my leg a little at a time.

PaPa even made me a wooden cane so I could hop around when I got tired of my chair with wheels. He scolded Nana, "You better take better care of yourself, old lady. Let Stara help you."

"No, I can do it myself, old man. She'll walk again, and soon! You'll see. When she returns to America, she'll walk off that boat to her Mommo. She'll be whole and healthy again. She's been sad and sick for too long."

"You're stubborn, old lady," he laughed. "What am I going to do with you? It's because of you that she even has her leg today."

NaNa had me slowly putting more and more weight on my leg while I used the cane. Little by little, I could feel myself getting stronger and stronger. "When you're ready to walk, we'll surprise everyone, Anna."

I'll never forget those months NaNa and I spent together. We sang together. We even completed crocheting our shawl together. I put it around her shoulders. "You look like a queen," I said. "Our shawl is beautiful. You can keep yourself warm and think of me when I'm gone."

"Oh, no, honey, it's yours to keep. It'll be a remembrance of the times we shared together...happy and sad. And now we need to prepare our surprise together."

When I walked for the first time, NaNa grabbed me and cried. "You look just like Baby when she tried to stand soon after she was born. I can finally rest now. My job is done." I didn't know what she meant when she said that I practiced walking for several days until my gait was steady enough that we could spring our surprise on everyone. After dinner one night when everyone finished eating, I surprised everyone by standing up from the table and

54

clearing the dishes.

"Look at Anna!" screamed Stryna Ann. "She's walking! You did it, NaNa!"

"No," she laughed, "Anna did it. She was the strong one. She's determined to go back home walking on two strong legs."

Everyone ran over to hug me and asked to see me walk some more. NaNa just sat there. I'll never forget the big grin on her face. She watched me like a mother bird watches her baby fly out of the nest for the first time. She winked at me as if to say, *we did it and my work is done.*

While everyone was getting ready for bed, NaNa got up to go to the outhouse.

"Can I go with you, NaNa?" I just wanted to be close to her for the rest of the night. This was a special night and I didn't want it to end. Nana had taken such good care of me, and now I wanted to care for her.

"Of course you can, but put on your coat, honey. It's cold outside."

"Okay, but I want you to put on our shawl to keep warm." I helped her wrap the shawl around her bony shoulders that stuck out like two sticks on her back. She was so small and the shawl so big, we laughed as we wrapped it around her twice.

It felt like the first winter snow would soon be upon us. The air was brisk. My nostrils stuck together between each breath. You could hear the cold hard ground crunching under our feet as we slowly walked to the outhouse. The smell of smoke curling up from the chimney brought the awareness that winter wasn't far behind. It was a clear night with a half-moon lighting our way. The stars were shining brightly. I watched NaNa swaying as she walked and I held on tight to steady her.

"It's my turn to hold your hand and help you walk," I laughed. We took our time. I held my arm around her tiny waist, making sure the shawl didn't touch the ground.

She was such a small woman that I was already taller than she. When we got there, I waited outside for her. I began counting the stars. The wind was blowing and I was getting pretty cold.

"NaNa, hurry up. It's getting cold out here." I continued counting more stars, but now my hands were getting numb. "NaNa, are you all right? I'm cold. I don't know how much longer I can wait." There was no answer. Finally, I opened the door to the outhouse. NaNa was slumped over with her eyes closed. I shook her real hard.

"NaNa, can you hear me?" Please answer me! Wake up!" I begged. Still NaNa didn't move. I ran, limping to the house and flung open the door screaming, "Come quick! Help! It's NaNa! PaPa, help me! Help NaNa! Hurry!"

The Funeral

NaNa's funeral day was dark and dreary. I didn't want her to be put into the cold ground, but PaPa said she was in heaven now and would never be cold again. All the women dressed in their colorful vests and wore black babushkas. The men and boys wore no hats.

In the cemetery in Pohorelá

NaNa's casket looked like Deddo's. It was brown with a white cover streaming over the side. Everything seemed so cold and hard as I looked at her lying there so still in that casket, which sat next to the hole dug for her burial. Somehow, this didn't suit her. She was like an angel: soft, warm and loving. As I stared at her face, frozen with a look that didn't become her, I wondered why I was always losing the people I loved the most. I asked PaPa if we could cover her with *our* shawl. I noticed he never took

57

his eyes off her the whole time we marched around her casket. We quietly said our prayers with the priest. Women prayed with their wooden rosaries and sang a beautiful song filled with sad hopes for her rise to heaven.

Before they closed the casket, PaPa took my hand and we walked over to NaNa for the last time. He carefully took the rosaries from her hands and placed them around my folded praying hands. Next, he carefully removed the shawl and wrapped it around my shoulders. I bent over her body, kissed her forehead and whispered in her cold, blue ear, "NaNa, I love you. Stay warm."

Before a funeral in Pohorelá, courtesy of Dr. Lubor Matejko, Comenius University in Slovak Republic

Everyone said NaNa kept her promise. She lived to see me walk again, and then needed to rest. If it had taken me longer to walk, maybe she would've lived longer...but I was happy my accident gave us the precious time we *did* have together.

When we got home, I wanted to be alone. I ran to the barn to be with Baby. PaPa found me crying in the barn. We spent quiet time just holding each other before he said anything.

"Honey, you and your Great-Grandma had some special times together. Even though her body has been buried in the ground, she'll always live on in your memories. She'll always be a part of you. Everything she taught you is alive in you. NaNa's spirit lives on in you, in Julia, in your Mommo, in all of us. Someday, you'll be a loving, caring mother and grandmother just like she was. Then you can teach your children and grandchildren what she taught you about life. It's okay to be sad. You'll miss her, but this sadness won't last forever. Just remember, she'll be with you wherever you are and whatever you're doing because her spirit is alive in you. Just because you can't see her doesn't mean she's not here with you."

Once again, PaPa and I just held each other for a long time before we went back into the house.

About two weeks after the funeral, Mommo wrote to us, saying that she had begun making arrangements with the government to obtain the necessary papers that would permit Julia and me to return to America.

I couldn't believe it might finally happen. Maybe NaNa was right. Maybe Mommo did love me. Maybe people do change. Mommo must've changed. She's sending for me. After five long years, I was finally going home.

Part Four:

The Long Trip Home

"*Oh, BaBa, do you still think about your NaNa?*" *asked Madison.*

"*All the time, dear. Everything she taught me is still alive in me. She taught me to have hope that people can change, to love my family and to believe in myself.*

"*Those are the things you always tell us to remember, too,*" *said Morgan.*

"*That's right. So even though you never met your Great-Great-Great-Great-Grandmother, things she taught me will now live on in the two of you. That's why telling my story to you every Thanksgiving is so important. These lessons will never be forgotten. She helped me understand that my Mommo's misfortunes weren't my fault after all, and that her love for me was always there.*"

"*Now I understand,*" *said Morgan. "The things you tell me came from your NaNa to my Grandma to my Dad to me. So that means your NaNa is alive in Madison and me!*"

Now you understand. My NaNa will live on forever in you, in your children and their children."

The girls cuddled even closer on BaBa's lap.

"*We love you, BaBa. We don't need any tissues for this part of your story, do we?*" *asked Madison.*

"*No, we don't and if we continue, we'll be able to hurry downstairs and join the family for another wonderful Thanksgiving dinner, sharing all the joys of our blessings.*"

Hello, America

There was a lot to do to prepare for our trip. Mommo sent information in her letters about all the arrangements and paperwork we needed. As long as we completed our health requirements, legal paperwork and paid our travel fees, everything would be fairly easy.

Otec read part of Mommo's letter to us:

> *"If John is certain he wants to come to America, everything will depend on Anna to make it happen. When you go to the government office, they'll want to assign a nurse to accompany the girls on the ship because they're too young to travel alone. Anna must cry and tell them she can't make the trip with a stranger. She must insist that her Stryk John go with her. She'll need to convince them that she's afraid to make the trip with a stranger. Since she's an American, they won't be able to refuse her."*

"Why me?" I cried. "I don't know if I can do that. That's a lie. I'm scared they won't believe me."

"You have to," said Stryk John. "That's the only way I'll be able to go too. Don't you want Stryna Ann, Johnny and Vernie to be with you some day?"

"Sure, I do."

"Well, then," said Otec, "I'll be with you when you talk to the government people. There's nothing to be scared about. We'll tell you exactly what you need to say. I'll be with you the whole time."

I could feel my stomach begin to ache. Otec patted my head as if to say that everything will work out okay. I wished I could be that sure.

Otec, Julia, Stryk John and I made the trip to the government office to receive all the instructions. When the officer began explaining that a nurse would have to make the trip with us, that was my cue to start crying.

The officer's lip was so stiff as he looked down at me and demanded, "A nurse must go with you and your sister. You cannot go alone."

"I can't go with a stranger," I cried. "I won't go."

"This child has been ill for six months," interrupted Otec. We just buried her Great-Grandma who nursed her back to health. She's in no position to travel with a stranger. Someone from the family must go with her and there's no one else except her Stryk John who can leave."

For some time there was disagreement about replacing the nurse with Stryk, but in the end, my uncontrollable tears worked.

The three of us eventually received a series of health shots to assure we would not bring any disease into America. Stara had a comb with narrow teeth that she used daily to comb our hair just to make sure we would pass the head lice inspection. Mommo warned us there would be doctors to examine us when we arrived in America. If we didn't pass their examination, we would be sent back to Europe. It was important we took care of every one of their requirements.

When it came time for us to finally leave, I said my goodbyes to Feathers, Pinky and Baby. Julia and I kissed and hugged Stryna Ann and the children. Lastly, we ran over to PaPa and Stara. I asked if we could say goodbye to NaNa. The four of us walked to the cemetery. I brought her some daisies. That was one of her favorite flowers. I knelt down and prayed my last goodbyes to her. Somehow I knew she was there with Julia and me. I felt her presence in my heart.

"It's time to go, Anna," said PaPa. "We don't want to be late getting you girls to the train on time."

As we walked away, I kept looking back over my shoulder at her grave. In the distance, the sun was shining on the mountains, giving a beautiful glow to the flowers and grass surrounding her grave. I would remember this picture forever.

We said our goodbyes to Otec as we boarded the train. The boat trip to America took about two long weeks. There were about five to six thousand passengers separated into four classes on the ship. There was first, second and third class. Then there was steerage. We were steerage. We had the lowest fares and were given the least desirable places to live at the bottom of the boat. We were all packed together into dark, damp, smelly compartments. We slept in narrow bunks stacked three high. Julia and I slept in the same bunk and covered ourselves with my shawl to keep warm. There were no showers, dining rooms or areas to play. If we wanted to roam about, we had to go up to the deck. Our food was served from huge kettles into metal dinner pails. I was seasick the whole time and couldn't even look at food. The sea never bothered Julia, but just looking and smelling food made me sick with the motion of the ship.

Stryk John had an idea for us to make some money during the trip. I dressed up in his clothes and tied a rope around the waist of his trousers. He drew a mustache on my face with charcoal. Julia wore a colorful vest, skirt and blouse. We danced and sang Slovak folk songs in the evenings for the passengers in the first and second-class dining rooms. They showed their enjoyment to our entertainment by throwing us money on the floor. We did this several times each week whenever I wasn't too seasick to perform.

We finally approached land in the distance. What a

thrill it was when we finally spotted the beautiful American symbol of freedom — the Statue of Liberty. The closer we got to her, the more everyone pointed, gasped, cried, danced and sang songs in many different languages.

Our boat anchored a short distance away from the coast of New York. The first and second-class passengers stayed on the boat to complete their medical and legal exams. The third class and steerage had to board another boat to get to Ellis Island. Before we did, they pinned identity tags on our clothing. Stryk kept complaining that he would've taken off his long johns if he had known how hot it was going to be.

The boat docked at a Hudson River pier at Ellis Island. That's where the examinations would occur. As we walked closer to the building, all we could hear were government men yelling, "Quick! Move along! Hurry!" in many different languages. There were hundreds of people filing into a large inspection hall. We all formed into single lines. Julia was restless and began roaming around the room, listening to people's conversations as long as they were speaking a language she understood. She came back to tell us stories.

"I heard people say we're going to be inspected. What does that mean?"

"Remember when your Mommo said they'll look at all our papers and examine our bodies to make sure we're healthy? That's what they mean by inspections," explained Stryk.

"Well, Anna doesn't look healthy," Julia whispered under her breath. "She's been seasick since we got on the boat. What if they want to send her back? They call Ellis Island 'Heartbreak Island' because of all the people they send back. When we climbed the steps to get to the examining room, I heard someone say that inspectors will be watching to see who's slow or looks unhealthy. Then they disqualify you and send you back. So, Anna, you better walk like you're feeling healthy."

Anna will be fine. Don't scare her," said Stryk.

I think Stryk was as scared as we were because his voice quivered as he spoke. I think everyone was scared of these examinations. Would they pass? Would they be sent back? Would everybody in their family pass together? If they did pass, what would be ahead of them in this strange land where they didn't even speak the language? They couldn't wait to see the golden streets.

It seemed forever until it was our turn to be examined. Mommo was right. They checked everything: our ears, eyes, hair. They sprayed our bodies to kill any bugs. There were two doctors. One completed the physical and mental examinations. The second one looked for signs of any contagious diseases that could be spread including the scalp, eyelids and skin. Anyone who required a more thorough examination was marked with chalk on their shoulder.

About twenty percent of all immigrants were held for additional questions of inspections. Those who passed went onto the next line where they were asked their name, nationality, occupation and if they could read or write. There were many interpreters there to assist the inspectors and immigrants with these questions. They asked how much money we had and where we were going. They kept a record of all that information.[9]

Finally, we left the inspection hall and boarded the ferryboat for New York. I looked across the water at the beautiful lady and vowed someday I would return and walk to the top of her torch.

When the ferryboat stopped, Stryk John, Julia and I held each other tightly as we stepped onto American soil. We did it! We made it! I dropped to my knees, kissed the ground and said *Daku Bogu, uz zych v Ameriki* (Thank you God, I'm in America)."

Epilogue

"**W**ell, girls, did you like hearing my story again?" I asked.

"You know we always do. I have a question, BaBa," said Morgan. "Why did people think the streets in America were lined with gold? I never saw gold on any streets."

"Years ago when Americans returned to their homelands across the sea, many times they had money to buy land or houses. They were considered to be successful and lucky in America. They also were more experienced and told unbelievable stories from the 'big world.' This was fascinating to their neighbors who knew nothing but the village where they lived and died. The men coming back from America usually didn't talk about the hard days and hard work they experienced in America. They only described life in America as a success story. The picture Slovak Americans painted to their friends and family in Czechoslovakia was only about the good times. Does that help you understand?"

"Yes."

"Just remember, girls, immigrants still come to America today from all parts of the world and for the same reason."

"What's that?" asked Morgan.

"They come to our country to seek a better life for themselves and their children."

"Now I have a question, BaBa," said Madison. "Did your dream about going back to New York and climbing all the way to the Statue of Liberty's torch ever come true?"

"You bet it did. That was one of the highlights of my life, girls."

They each gave BaBa one last embrace. Madison then

grabbed BaBa's hand and walker and said, "I think it's time we better go downstairs."

"You're right! It's time to join the family for another happy Thanksgiving!"

Madison, Anna and Morgan

Glossary

Amputate –To surgically remove a diseased limb or other part of the body

Animated – To make or design in such a way as to create apparently spontaneous lifelike movement.

Assisted Living Complex –A facility housing and caring for senior citizens.

BaBa –An endearing word Morgan and Madison called their Great-Grandmother.

Blast Furnace – A furnace in which combustion is forced by current of air under pressure especially for the reduction of iron ore.

Bumper Crop – A plentiful harvest of a particular type of plant.

Culture – Characteristics and beliefs that are distinctive and/or unique to a particular group of people

Delirious – A mental disturbance characterized by confusion, disordered speech and hallucinations.

First Holy Communion - A Catholic ceremony during which new members of the church receive the holy sacrament for the first time.

Gnarly - To twist into a state of deformity.

Gossip – To speak, often in an unflattering manner, about other people and private matters in their lives

Hungary – A European country bordering to the south of Slovakia.

Intellectuals – A person who is devoted to study and knowledge.

Intuitive – A person possessing quick and ready insight

Landlocked – Enclosed by land.

Magyars – A dominant people of the country of Hungary.

Outhouse – A small structure, located outdoors, that is used as a bathroom

Pasturage – Plants grown especially for the feeding of animals.

Reprimand – To scold someone for saying or doing something that had a negative outcome

Sallow – A grayish, greenish, yellow color.

Sepia – A brownish gray to a dark olive brown.

Sniper – To shoot at exposed people from a hidden vantage point.

Stride – To take very long steps.

Tenants – One who rents property.

Visa – Formal approval made by proper authorities giving permission to proceed.

Widow – A woman who has lost her husband by death.

End Notes

[1] Slovak words containing "j" sound like "y"

[2] "A Search For Freedom." Alexander Kobulsky. Slovak Garden Scholarship Contestant. 2003. 27 January 2003. *http://www.slovakgarden.com*

[3] ibid. Kobulsky. *http://www.slovakgarden.com*

[4] ibid. Kobulsky. *http://www.slovakgarden.com*

[5] Billings, Molly. "The Influenza Pandemic of 1918." Virus. Group. Modified RDS, June, 1997. Stanford University. February, 2005. *http://www.stanford.edu*

[6] Summary. History. Slovakia. Countries. *http://www.geographyig.com*

[7] *"19th Century."* Slovakia. History. The Guide to the Slovakia Republic. *http://www.slovakia.org*

[8] *"20th Century."* Slovakia. History. The Guide to the Slovkia Republic. *http://www.slovakia.org*

[9] Freidman, Russell. *Immigrant Kids.* Puffin Books, 1995.